THE KNOPF POETRY SERIES

1 Robert Mazzocco, *Trader*

2 Cynthia Macdonald, *(W)holes*

3 Thomas Rabbitt, *The Booth Interstate*

4 Edward Hirsch, *For the Sleepwalkers*

5 Marie Ponsot, *Admit Impediment*

6 Brad Leithauser, *Hundreds of Fireflies*

7 Katha Pollitt, *Antarctic Traveller*

8 Nicholas Christopher, *On Tour with Rita*

9 Amy Clampitt, *The Kingfisher*

10 Alan Williamson, *Presence*

11 Stephen Sandy, *Riding to Greylock*

12 Pamela White Hadas, *Beside Herself*

13 Sharon Olds, *The Dead and the Living*

14 Peter Klappert, *The Idiot Princess of the Last Dynasty*

15 Mary Jo Salter, *Henry Purcell in Japan*

16 Norman Williams, *The Unlovely Child*

17 Marilyn Hacker, *Assumptions*

Also by Marilyn Hacker

PRESENTATION PIECE

SEPARATIONS

TAKING NOTICE

ASSUMPTIONS

ASSUMPTIONS

Marilyn Hacker

ALFRED A. KNOPF   NEW YORK   1985

THIS IS A BORZOI BOOK
PUBLISHED BY ALFRED A. KNOPF, INC.

"Letters from the Alpes Maritimes," "Fourteen," and "Days of 1959" were
originally published in *Feminist Studies*. "Two Young Women" first
appeared in *Frontiers: A Journal of Women Studies*. "A Chaplet for Judith
Landry" and "Gerda in the Eyrie" were first published in *Poetry*.

Grateful acknowledgment is given to the editors of the following periodi-
cals, in which other poems in this volume first appeared: *Ambit, Bananas,
Chelsea, Conditions, The London Magazine, The Missouri Review, New
England Review and Bread Loaf Quarterly, No Apologies, Ploughshares,
Prairie Schooner, Shenandoah, Sinister Wisdom*, and *Thirteenth Moon*.

Library of Congress Cataloging in Publication Data
Hacker, Marilyn
    Assumptions.
    (Knopf poetry series ; 17)
    I. Title.
PS3558.A28A9   1985   811'.54   84–48537
ISBN 0–394–54229–0
ISBN 0–394–72826–2 (pbk.)

Manufactured in the United States of America
FIRST EDITION

With sincere thanks to the MacDowell Colony, the Michael Karolyi Memorial Foundation, the Ossabaw Foundation, the Corporation of Yaddo, the New York State Creative Artists Public Service Grants, and the John Simon Guggenheim Foundation, for providing the space and the time in which much of this book was written.

CONTENTS

LETTER FROM THE ALPES-MARITIMES   I

INHERITANCES   9
Towards Autumn   11
Two Young Women   13
Almost Aubade   14
Fourteen   15
Mother   16
Days of 1959   17
Fifteen to Eighteen   18
1973   19
Mother II   20
Autumn 1980   22
Part of a True Story   25
A Chaplet for Judith Landry   29
Sword   32
Inheritances   33
Joint Custody   35

OPEN WINDOWS   37

GRAFFITI FROM THE GARE SAINT-MANQUÉ   53

THE SNOW QUEEN   63
The Witch's Garden   65
What the Tame Crow Sang to Gerda   67
Gerda in the Eyrie   68

The Robber Woman   73
The Little Robber Girl Considers the Wide World   76
Rune of the Finland Woman   78
The Little Robber Girl Gets On in the Wide World   80
The Little Robber Girl Considers Some Options   85

BALLAD OF LADIES LOST AND FOUND   87

LETTER FROM THE
ALPES-MARITIMES

LETTER FROM THE ALPES-MARITIMES

I.M. James A. Wright

Carissima Joannissima, *ave,*
from a deceptively apolitical
solitude. (Must I be auto-critical,
having exchanged upper-Manhattan Soave
for Côtes de Provence?)

In this cottage with light on four sides I shared
for a conjugal fortnight three years ago,
I play the housewife-hermit, putter. I know
the pots, the plates, the water-heater. My third
midsummer in Vence

whose suburban villas fructify the hills
out the kitchen window, my perimeter
marked by an ivy-cloaked oak. Out the French door,
yellow exclamations of broom in scrub-wild
haphazard descent

down ancient rock-terraces to the ravine
where a cold brook sings, loud as the nightingale's
liquid vespers. When you go down the woods trail
to the water, it's a surprise to find
such small source for song.

I watch the sky instead of television.
Weather comes south over the mountains: that's news.
Today the Col de Vence was crystalline. Blues
stratospheric and Mediterranean
in the direction

of Nice. From Tourrettes, I could see Corsica.
Sometimes I take myself out to dinner. I write
between courses, in a garden, where twilight
softens the traffic beyond the begonias,
and my pichet, *vin*

ordinaire, but better than ordinary,
loosens my pen instead of tongue; not my guard.
I like eating alone; custom makes it hard
to be perceived content though solitary.
A woman alone

must know how to be cautious when she gets drunk.
I can't go rambling in night fields of horses,
apostrophizing my wine to their apples,
heaving an empty with a resounding thunk
in someone's garden.

Nor are, yet, establishments for grape and grain
the frequent settings for our lucky meetings.
I think of you, near other mountains, eating
breakfast, or warming the car up in the rain
to do your errands.

Both of us are happy in marketplaces.
In your letter, bargains at J. C. Penney's.
I'm in the town square early. Crowded Friday's
cheese-sellers and used-clothes vendors know my face's
regular seasons.

Djuna Barnes and the Equal Rights Amendment
died in the same month. Though there's a party Sunday,
why should I celebrate the Fourth of July?
Independence? No celebration without
Representation.

The exotic novel Barnes could have written
continues here: the old Countess and her child,
further than ever from being reconciled,
warily, formally, circle the old bone:
an inheritance.

Between mother and daughter I'd be a bone,
too. I cultivate pleasant neutrality,
reassuring each of them she can trust my
discretion, though I think they both know my own
clear preferences.

I gave the mother a blood-red gloxinia.
Hothouse perennial herself at ninety,
terrible on the roads (Countess Báthory
is rumored to be a direct ancestor),
a war monument's

long bones, selective eyes, a burnished ruin
in white jeans, along the lines of Katharine
Hepburn around the cheekbones and vulpine chin,
her style half-diplomacy, half-flirtation:
she gets what she wants;

which is what her daughter has never gotten:
bad marriage, penury, a retarded son,
father's sublime indifference and mother's scorn.
She's sixty-two now, and accused of plotting
"under influence

of a bad woman." That they are two old dears
goes without saying, and that daughter loves her
friend, but, *avec amour,* her wicked mother.
Add that one of them was a French officer,
one an ambulance

driver in the War, and that the property
where I live is the object of contention,
and that the penniless daughter is as handsome
as the mother who'd will her patrimony
to the state of France.

I'm thirty-nine and thin again, hair thinning
too, *hélas,* as when, in London, twenty-nine,
I paid a trichologist, wore long skirts, pined
in a Park Road bed-sit, and read, through waning
light, anti-romance

by Ivy Compton-Burnett, hoping to lose
(my American soul?) San Francisco–style
expectations, though the Sixties were a while
over. I didn't know I could change and choose
another ambiance.

Better celibate than a back-street girlfriend.
(I called myself that, ironic in self-scorn,
waiting for evasive letters across town.)
I know I'll never have to do that again.
At least two women

at least a while loved me reciprocally.
That I knew I could love them, I owe to you.
I see tomorrow's weather from the window.
I've found my spot—the kitchen, naturally.
I've put basil plants

in an orange juice jar to root. Though I said
I went wistfully under the flowering May
boughs in Central Park, single, while pairs of my
friends blissed out in rut, I don't think that I need
antidepressants!

I don't think I'm even frequently depressed
without the old objective correlative.
Perhaps I am as skinless and sensitive
—"sensitive"'s necessary—as you suggest.
Long-sleeved elephant's

hide coveralls I metaphorically wore
that month of committees, trysting visitors,
arrivals, entertainments and departures.
I can write poetry now, if I don't bore
the constituents

who never read it, though they all want to Write
Something. In all fairness, I'm not being fair.
Hendecasyllabics, Joannissima,
could ramble on for forty-three days and nights
until I leave France.

I'll stop, hoping to see you in October
face to face, with help from universities.
(Here, a wordplay on "tenure" and "liberty.")
"Long bones," recalls you, too, once almost my lover,
happily my friend.

INHERITANCES

TOWARDS AUTUMN

Mid-September, and I miss my daughter.
I sit out on the terrace with my friend,
talking, with morning tea, coffee, and bread,
about another woman, and her mother,
who survived heroism; her lover
who will have to. I surprise myself

with language; lacking it, don't like myself
much. I owe a letter to my daughter.
Thinking of her's like thinking of a lover
I hope will someday grow to be a friend.
I missed the words to make friends with my mother.
I pull the long knife through the mound of bread,

spoon my slice with cherry preserves, the bread
chewy as meat beneath, remind myself
I've errands for our ancient patron, mother
of dramas, hard mother to a daughter
twenty years my senior, who is my friend,
who lives in exile with a woman lover

also my friend, three miles from here. A lover
of good bread, my (present) friend leaves this bread
and marmalades *biscottes*. To have a friend

a generation older than myself
is sometimes like a letter for my daughter
to read, when she can read: What your mother

left undone, women who are not your mother
may do. Women who are not your lover
love you. (That's to myself, and my daughter.)
We take coffee- and tea-pot, mugs, jam jars, bread
inside, wash up. I've work, hours by myself.
Beyond the kitchen, in her room, my friend

writes, overlooking the same hills. Befriend
yourself: I couldn't have known to tell my mother
that, unless I'd learned it for myself.
Until I do. Friendship is earned. A lover
leaps into faith. Earthbound women share bread;
make; do. Cherry compote would please my daughter.

My daughter was born hero to her mother;
found, like a lover, flawed; found, like a friend,
faithful as bread I'd learn to make myself.

TWO YOUNG WOMEN

Vence: forenoon bells for the fifteenth of August;
sunlight; circular tin café table.
They are quarreling about their mothers.
They have been to Mass: the Assumption
of Mary moves certain unbelievers.
Pedantic sermon in pedantic French,
but they exchanged the kiss of peace with
elderly Frenchwomen on either side.
Aquatic lightfall through Matisse stained glass
was beautiful. They are beautiful
with morning catching in their clean short hair,
but one could stay here with her friend forever
(imagines it: she has a job, a child);
one misses her loft, her other lover;
(in fact, they both are gluttonous for letters)
so they are quarreling about their mothers:
ought they condemn, forgive, their own, each other's
mother (never met) for delivering
them, fragile and untrusting, to each other?

ALMOST AUBADE

The little hours: two lovers herd upstairs
two children, one of whom is one of theirs.
Past them, two of the other sex lope down,
dressed for mid-winter cruising bars in brown
bomber-jackets—their lives as uncluttered
as their pink shaven cheeks, one of us muttered,
fumbling with keys. Yes, they did look alike.
Hooking their scarves and parkas on the bike,
the seven-year-old women shuck a heap
of velvet jeans and Mary Janes. They sleep
diagonal, instantly, across the top
bunk, while their exhausted elders drop,
not to the bliss breasts melt to against breasts
yet, but to kitchen chairs. One interests
herself in omelets, listening anyhow.
It's certain that fine women pick at food.
A loaf of bread, a jug of wine, and thou
shalt piecemeal total both, gripped in that mood
whose hunger makes a contrapuntal stutter
across connectives. Unwrap cheese, find butter,
dip bread crusts in a bowl of pasta sauce
saved from the children's supper. Tired because
of all we should stay up to say, we keep
awake together often as we sleep
together. I'll clear the plates. Leave your cup.
Lie in my arms until the kids get up.

FOURTEEN

We shopped for dresses which were always wrong:
sweatshop approximations of the lean-
lined girls' wear I studied in *Seventeen*.
The armholes pinched, the belt didn't belong,
the skirt drooped forward (I'd be told at school).
Our odd-lot bargains deformed the image,
but she and I loved Saturday rummage.
One day she listed outside Loehmann's. Drool
wet her chin. Stumbling, she screamed at me. Dropping
our parcels on the pavement, she fell in
what looked like a fit. I guessed: Insulin.
The cop said, "Drunk," and called an ambulance
while she cursed me and slapped away my hands.
When I need a mother, I still go shopping.

MOTHER

I was born when she was thirty-eight.
Pleated secrets sunlit on a skirt
spread over rocks, dark curls, sharp nose, alert
shopgirl's cautious mouth-curve. She had to wait
between high school and college, married late
—thirty-one—motherless teen-aged, serving
father, time black-frocked at Macy's, deserving
Jewish daughter. Patience: her great
longings encysted with it, burst. I'll be
thirty-eight in November. In her head
whir words she learned, memorized, accented
impeccably out of the Bronx. In the Bronx she
rages, shrunken, pillow-propped, in a rank
room. I invent freedom at the bank.

I invent stories she will never tell.
I was fatherless; she was motherless.
I thought that I was motherless as well.
Harridan, pincurled in a washed-out housedress,
she scrubbed the tiny kitchen on all fours
and sniped. I bolted. I told dog-walkers,
as I chipped bark flakes from the sycamore
out front, such stories! I do not know hers.
The mother says, "When I was twenty, I . . ."
The daughter, "I was . . . I never thought you . . ."
"My best friend . . ." "I was afraid. Tell me why . . . ?"
". . . I was afraid." Twined down the long wind go
fictions, afternoon lies the nurse tells to
a furious old woman, who will die.

DAYS OF 1959

He had devirginated my friend Nan.
Nuyorican, gorgeous, all parts made small,
he was married to a round-shouldered, tall-
er-than-he-was WASP science-fiction fan,
a saccharine-frosted Lauren Bacall
who filed while "Le Théâtre du Vingtième
Siècle" caused my proximity to him.
I knew enough to be a know-it-all
maiden adulteress with diaphragm
in their East Third St. bed before midterm.
"Starbright, I hope I have someone like you
to love me when I'm fifty." He didn't mean
me; he meant, some girl under eighteen.
Somewhere or other, he is fifty now.

He's fifty somewhere now; perhaps he has;
unless the dope that he commenced to do
at twenty-five did him. Sartre and jazz
played into idiot opiates, right out
of that South Bronx he never talked about.
He left his wife, but she was shooting too,
by then. Once his initiate in grass,
I was a has-been hanger-on, ignored
uptown in all-night diners while he scored,
then "A" down, West Bronx "D" back home, lone Jew-
ess on the milk train; south to class
next day, badly prepared except to doubt
practically anything anyone knew.
I snorted once; was, by some blessing, bored.

FIFTEEN TO EIGHTEEN

I'd almost know, the nights I snuck in late,
at two, at three, as soon as I had tucked
into myself tucked in, to masturbate
and make happen what hadn't when I fucked,
there'd be the gargled cry, always "God damn
you to hell," to start with, from the other
bedroom: she was in shock again. I swam
to my surface to take care of my mother.
That meant, run for a glass of orange juice,
clamp her shoulders with one arm, try to pour
it down her throat while she screamed, "No, God damn
you!" She is stronger than I am
when this happens. If she rolls off on the floor,
I can't / she won't let me / lift her up. Fructose
solution, a shot and she'd come around.
At half-past-two, what doctor could I call?
Sometimes I had to call the hospital.
More often, enough orange juice got down,
splashed on us both.
                              "What are you doing here?
Where were you? Why is my bed in this mess?
How did you get those scratches on your face?
What were you doing, out until this hour?"

1973

"I'm pregnant," I wrote to her in delight
from London, thirty, married, in print. A fools-
cap sheet scrawled slantwise with one minuscule
sentence came back. "I hope your child is white."
I couldn't tear the pieces small enough.
I hoped she'd be black as the ace of spades,
though hybrid beige heredity had made
that as unlikely as the spun-gold stuff
sprouted after her neo-natal fur.
I grudgingly acknowledged her "good hair,"
which wasn't, very, from my point of view.
"No tar-brush left," her father's mother said.
"She's Jewish and she's white," from her cranked bed
mine smugly snapped.
                              She's Black. She is a Jew.

MOTHER II

No one is "Woman" to another
woman, except her mother.
Her breasts were unmysterious
naked: limp, small. But I thought pus
must ooze from them: her underwear
like bandages. Blood came from where
I came from, stanched with pads between
her legs, under the girdle, seen
through gaping bathroom doors. Around
her waist, all sorts of rubber. Bound
to stop the milk, my milk, her breasts
stayed flat. I watched my round self, guessed
a future where I'd droop and leak.
But dry and cool against her cheek
I'd lean my cheek. I stroked the lace
and serge she sheathed her carapace
with: straight skirts, close cuffs, full sleeves;
was, wordless, catechized; believed:
nude, she was gaunt; dressed, she was slim;
nude, she was flabby; dressed, her firm
body matched her brisk, precise
mid-continental teacher's voice,
which she had molded, dry, perfect-
ed from a swamp of dialect.
Naked or clad, for me, she wore
her gender, perpetual *chador,*

her individual complex
history curtained off by sex.
Child, I determined that I would
not be subsumed in womanhood.
Whatever she was, I was not.
Whoever she was, I forgot
to ask, and she forgot to tell,
muffled in costumes she as well
rejected as a girl, resumed
—on my account? Are women doomed,
beasts that repeat ourselves, to rage
in youth against our own old age,
in age to circumscribe our youth
with self-despisal dressed as truth?
Am I "Woman" to my water-
dwelling brown loquacious daughter,
corporeal exemplar of
her thirst for what she would not love?

AUTUMN 1980
for Judith McDaniel

I spent the night after my mother died
in a farmhouse north of Saratoga Springs
belonging to a thirty-nine-year-old
professor with long, silvered wiry hair,
a lively girl's flushed cheeks and gemstone eyes.
I didn't know that she had died.
Two big bitches and a varying
heap of cats snoozed near a black wood stove
on a rag rug, while, on the spring-shot couch
we talked late over slow glasses of wine.
In the spare room near Saratoga Springs
was a high box bed. My mother died
that morning, of heart failure, finally.
Insulin shocks burned out her memory.
On the bed, a blue early-century
Texas Star, in a room white and blue
as my flannel pajamas. I'd have worn
the same, but smaller, ten years old at home.
Home was the Bronx, on Eastburn Avenue,
miles south of the hermetic not-quite-new
block where they'd sent this morning's ambulance.
Her nurse had telephoned. My coat was on,
my book-stuffed bag already on my back.
She said, "Your mother had another shock.
We'll be taking her to the hospital."
I asked if I should stay. She said, "It's all
right." I named the upstate college where

I'd speak that night. This had happened before.
I knew / I didn't know: it's not the same.
November cold was in that corner room
upstairs, with a frame window over land
the woman and another woman owned
—who was away. I thought of her alone
in her wide old bed, me in mine. I turned
the covers back. I didn't know she had died.
The tan dog chased cats; she had to be tied
in the front yard while I went along
on morning errands until, back in town,
I'd catch my bus. November hills were raw
fall after celebratory fall
foliage, reunions, festival.
I blew warmth on my hands in a dark barn
where two shaggy mares whuffled in straw,
dipped steaming velvet muzzles to the pail
of feed. We'd left the pickup's heater on.
It smelled like kapok when we climbed inside.
We both unzipped our parkas for the ride
back to the Saratoga bus station.
I blamed the wind if I felt something wrong.
A shrunken-souled old woman whom I saw
once a month lay on a hospital
slab in the Bronx. Mean or not, that soul
in its cortège of history was gone.
I didn't know that I could never know,

now, the daughtering magic to recall
across two coffee-mugs the clever Young
Socialist whose views would coincide
with mine. I didn't know that she had died.
Not talking much, while weighted sky pressed down,
we climbed the back road's bosom to the all-
night diner doubling as a bus depot.
I brushed my new friend's cool cheek with my own,
and caught the southbound bus from Montreal.
I counted boarded-up racetrack motel
after motel. I couldn't read. I tried
to sleep. I didn't know that she had died.
Hours later, outside Port Authority,
rained on, I zipped and hooded an obscure
ache from my right temple down my shoulder.
Anonymous in the mid-afternoon
crowds, I'd walk, to stretch, I thought, downtown.
I rode on the female wave, typically
into Macy's (where forty-five years
past, qualified by her new M.A.
in Chemistry, she'd sold Fine Lingerie),
to browse in Fall Sale bargains for my child,
aged six, size eight, hung brilliantly or piled
like autumn foliage I'd missed somehow,
and knew what I officially didn't know
and put the bright thing down, scalded with tears.

PART OF A TRUE STORY
for Margaret Delany

"*We dress* UP!"—Ntozake Shange

My dear Mrs. Bloomer:
                    The exigencies
of my life demand rational costume.
I noticed recently upon perusal
of a number of your interesting
journal, *The Lily,* that your radical
bifurcate garment for gentlewomen
is beyond suggestion; not to mince words,
for sale.
         My people, Mrs. Bloomer, are
as well, south of the District, and until
the last and least of us no longer is
chattel, this woman must be radical
to be rational. A woman of color
is gentle as yourself, until provoked.
I have been, since the age of six.
                              When I,
aged twenty-some, returned to the scene
of my truncated childhood, with the goal
—which I achieved—of bringing forth my mother
and my father from bondage, as I had
my brothers, many of my sisters and
brothers, I was obliged, for my safety
and theirs, to come to them in male attire.
(Does *attire* have gender?) I cannot pass
as other than I am in one respect;

nor would I wish to. It was curious
passing that other way, where I had passed
before: "This gal can haul as heavy a
load as three men or a mule," et cetera.
A black man is only marginally
more anonymous on a Southern road
than a black woman. Dare I confess, I
liked that marginal anonymity?
Crop-headed in a neutral suit of clothes,
I sat, a stranger at my mother's table,
bearing good news she could not bear to hear
who bore me, till I bared myself as well,
scarred as I was, to loving scrutiny.
Later, I also bore the scrutiny
of the spouse whom I had reluctantly
left; who, free, had forbidden me to go
to freedom. Newly wived, he did not know
me at all, either as woman, or as
myself. It's a peculiar thing: to pass
easily, anonymously, from one
life, or mode of life, to another: done
with a forked suit? Night, starvation, a gun
to scare stragglers to courage, sleep in snow
or straw or not at all are what I know
as passage-rites. I do what I can,
but I do not wish to be thought a man
again.

      Tonight, four hundred human souls,
still embodied, disembondaged, lie wakeful

or sleep in this rough but hospitable
hospice, this time, taken across water
to free land. You know the name I am called.
The straits do not. We cross them nonetheless.
I have another name now: General;
a task I had first as a nursling: Nurse.
We intend to bring out four hundred more.
I wish to be there. It is efficacious
that I be there. I must be recognized
though: black, female, and old, or nearly old.
Still, I am of scant use immobilized.
I wish to be relieved of the woolen gown
whose waterlogged skirts and underskirts hold
me so, as well as the Confederate
Army would wish. I was nearly drowned.
Thus, Mrs. Bloomer, my request. Disguise
is not wished, or called for. Compromise,
though unaccustomed, is appropriate
on this occasion. So is the connection
of our aims. I entertain reflection
that, free and black, I am still disfranchised,
female; a condition I first realized
espoused: bondwoman and freedman, we
embodied it. I transcend limitation.
I am a black woman, whose education
was late and little: necessity
of adulthood vowed to emancipation
of my people; the larger limitation
imposed by childhood spent in servitude,

leave me comparatively unlettered.
You will receive this missive, dictated
by me to my adjutant, from her
hand, to which I pray you will deliver
the costume I desire.

Awaiting your

kind reply, I remain,

Yours faithfully,

Harriet Tubman   United States Army
Medical Division   Port Royal Island

Port Royal Island was captured from the Confederacy by the Union Army in 1861, and became a haven for escaped slaves. Harriet Tubman, then aged about forty-one, and the most successful—and hunted—conductor on the Underground Railroad, was sent there by the governor of Massachusetts in 1862. She served as an Army scout, and as a nurse and herbal healer in the field hospital established for the freed slaves and wounded soldiers. In 1863 she led a detachment of the Second South Carolina Volunteers, a company composed of black soldiers under the command of Colonel James Montgomery, in a raid up the Combahee River, with the objectives of destroying the torpedoes with which the Confederate Army had mined the river, and of liberating as many slaves from the coastal farms as could be transported to Port Royal on the gunboats. More than eight hundred were freed. Harriet Tubman thus added the sobriquet "General" to the name of Moses, by which even her commanding officer addressed her.

Shortly afterwards, Tubman, who had never learned to read and write, dictated a letter to Boston, ordering a Bloomer suit, because long skirts were a handicap on such a campaign.

Amelia Bloomer, feminist, abolitionist, and originator of the costume which bore her name, was also editor of *The Lily*, a periodical advocating women's rights.

I'd like to express my gratitude to Ann Petry for her biography of Harriet Tubman; its concise information fueled my imagination.

A CHAPLET FOR JUDITH LANDRY

Dear Judith: In sincerest gratitude,
here is the bread-and-butter gift requested.
I wouldn't want our friendship to be tested
because I didn't sit down and get at it. "Rude
and slovenly, with a bad attitude,"
you'd say; although there might be worse things listed
against me if my offering consisted
of cliché justified by platitude.
I'm writing to you from an estuarial
island, where deer graze, pigs rampage, loons sing; land
marsh-bottomed, oyster-bedded, territorial
range of wild horses, freed pets' progeny.
But still I close my eyes and think of England:
where else could we dig into Kedgeree?

Where else could we dig into Kedgeree
with a prolific writer who'd just been
presented, after sherry, to the Queen?
(Next time they meet, she'll be a C.B.E.)
Two raw colonials, my girl and me
quivered respectfully, thrilled to the bone.
That's why we put on everything we owned,
although it was a sultry fifty-three
indoors. To sit by the electric fire,
stroking enchanting Rock-cake, gone quite flat
(sign of advanced achievement in a cat),

and sip Frascati—I could not desire
more! While our natterings didn't dislodge
from the kittens! the kittens! enraptured Squodge.

From the kittens! the kittens! enraptured Squodge
could only be occasionally pried.
(Say, if a Hamley's van pulled up outside,
sent by the Queen, *pour rendre ses hommages.*)
I'm sorry if we left a grubby hodge-
podge of Lego, socks and tracts beside
your easy-chair. We're sloppy, but we tried
to be acceptably contained and *sages.*
I liked the Oriental rugs beneath
and upon the table where we ate,
watching daffodils bloom in the teeth
of London bluster beyond French windows.
You liked loud Iva who resists repose.
I liked tall Lurky who stays up too late.

I liked tall Lurky who stays up too late,
although I missed the threatened saxophone
rehearsal. Living, equals, with your grown
daughter, you enlighten me and my eight-
year-old, who've witnessed pairs wasting with hate-
ful wrangling, while we hug and spar our own
infatuation. You were kind to loan
me your featherbed. Under its weight,

I slept like a ploughman with my socks on.
Mornings we drank hot coffee-milk from bowls.
The Saturday it rained, we vetoed Kew
and herded Iva, via the Number 2
to look, with Bonnard (recognition shocks) on
interiors domestic as our souls.

Interiors domestic as our souls,
salvaged like postcards of congenial places:
frayed armchairs framing animated faces,
the two-bar fire with fake electric coals.
The kamikaze boys'-club that controls
just the survival of the human race is
excluded temporarily. What grace is
implicit in our customary roles
—confidante, chatelaine, cook, hostess, mother—
when, our own women, we have latitude
to choose them and enact them for each other.
Our homes very infrequently are castles.
Having shared yours, we'll pledge ourselves your vassals,
dear Judith, in sincerest gratitude.

SWORD
for Toi Derricotte

This golden vengeance is one of those red
niggers like her grandfather who said
of me, "Her people are just off the boat."
He might have said, just off the cattle cars.
Here she is three, bangs her construction boot
against the van she's perched on. He is in lace,
held by a darker nurse, sixty-six years
earlier. Their twice-bright blade of face
astonishes, doubled, between imp ears
the same red-gold (his lock's glassed) curls around.
When she was born he was long darkened; dead
before he tried her honed red-gold, hybrid
of six million dead off the cattle cars,
just off the slave boats, fifteen million drowned.

INHERITANCES

Iva asks me for stories of her father's
family. I learned them second-hand
—not even a Christian, and not black.
I think of a reflective membrane: classes,
mirrored, meld. She starts with slavery.
The eight-year-old hunkered in the old man's

barrel-staves to hide when the blue horseman
(she breathed in horse) leaned toward her grandfather
to shout, "Old man, you're free!" While slavery
had slipped, a wristlet from the writing-hand
of the bisque-beige girl enrolled in Classes
for Young Ladies, in Paris, where her black

mother was not. Ledgers were in the black;
the permeated membrane not the man,
else childless, who exercised three classes'
prerogatives (landed, white, male) to father
twice the child who, by his power in hand,
was bred to, and released from, slavery.

Iva asks, "Were your parents *for* slavery?
Were *they* slaves? I know they weren't black."
She puts her suntanned hand against my hand,

compares. "Does 'manumit' mean, just a man
could make slaves free?" I tell her, my father
spoke German in his West Bronx first-grade classes;

my mother worked at Macy's, took night classes
at Hunter, read about Wage Slavery
and Profits in the kitchen, where her father
waited for her to make his breakfast. Black
dresses were required for work. A man
—Jewish, of course—would take her life in hand.

I don't wear any rings on my left hand.
Two copies of notes home from Iva's classes
are sent. Her father lives with a white man,
writes science-fiction novels: slavery
on far worlds, often, though the slaves aren't black.
She says, "Dad's roommate," or "My other father."

I wouldn't say to a black friend that class is
(in its erasures) slavery. I hand
down little to emancipate my father.

JOINT CUSTODY

Houston was unregenerately damp
—clouds scudded in, clouds scudded out with rain—
and quintessentially American
as neon reindeer in a trailer camp.
Nobody else was a pedestrian
on boulevards of monkey-puzzle trees.
Conventual in lodgings, with no forced
festival, we watched the landlady
unwrap things her grown son passed to her knees.
Like us, she was a teacher and divorced.
There was a story: he, now tranquilized
and nelly, stabbed her with a kitchen knife.
Latterly, a boyfriend and nightlife
helped. They both exhausted their surprised
exclamations at a magnetized
ceramic apple, a red calico
apple, a crystal apple ornament,
a box of apple-printed notecards, sent
by kindergarten mothers. I had no
proof of parental status for the Show
and Tell, but missed my child so much it hurt
—who held, swathed in yards of new organdy,

Christmas court for her father's family.
Pushing aside an iced wedge of inert
factory buns, I passed my spinsterly
book-parcel across cushions in a lull,
to be revealed, requited, by my dear
friend, equally a displaced person here,
compassionate, impeccable in wool
challis, and (maybe) just as miserable.

OPEN WINDOWS

1

This isn't about unrequited love
although I'm warmed by your proximity.
I don't yearn for you, wish you wanted me
a different way. I want you to approve
my life, my person: insecurity
hamstrings me without reassuring strokes.
Earned trust some careless clumsiness revokes,
some fervid overstatement nullifies:
that's happened. When I'm with you, something ties
me to your mood, should not. You're not my child.
I think of feeling absolutely free
outside the Gare Routière, in a blue-tiled
café, alone in France, morning haze, mild
light in my brown hands, cupping it like a prize.

2

Tonight when I cup my hand beneath your breast
(fountain and pillow of felicity)
your womb shudders with possibility
suctioned from you, and your sigh is pain. Pressed
even gently against me, you ache; the best
choice, made, presses us both. How will it be
held between us, this complicity
in what we can't repeat? Silken, we nest
aloft, sleep curled. Reflected from the snow,
a dawn lamp glints up through your tall window.
Uptown, my child will wake, ask where's her mother.
Promised, I inhale you, descend from you, gather
scattered woolens, gather my wits to go
from one hard choice, love chosen, to the other.

3
for Sára Karig

On the back of a letter in French applying
for a place at a bilingual school for my daughter
I put words that will not contain the slaughter
of somebody's twenty-year-old. She is dying
under a modern airport where the roar
of takeoffs flattens screams and retching to blurred
industrial noise around the torturer.
Below the tiled floor is the dirt floor.
A woman is living whose name I say like a charm
because she acknowledged choice in the dulled eyes
of somebody's son, who, needled to recognize
a congruent soul in the law student or farm
child he is reducing to an integer
of shamed pain, would be stripped and killed with her.

4

While deathdrunk superannuated boys
tot up how often to blow up the world,
a white-locked pink sage with a toddler voice
recounts, purse clutched, how she was blued and curled.
I overhear her on the crosstown bus
I take at three to meet the second grade.
She smiles a smile someone called dangerous
once, and she boiled it down like marmalade.
I'm sheared, hands free, with keys, jackknife and ten
dollars deployed in worn corduroy pants.
A matrifocal world would comprehend
compassion, dignity and commonsense,
I sneer, aware of my accoutrements
as she is talking hairdos with her friend.

5

"You'll play with *her,* but you won't play with *me!*"
my lover snapped, gathering up her beach-
mat after her as she scuffed angrily
back toward the car. She turned, we glowered at each
other. Play with my child's part of my work:
loved work, but work. I thought she understood,
after our harried winter in New York,
I'd need an afternoon of solitude
precisely when that work was imminent.
She's going to cry again. This isn't real!
"I *have*" (icily) "other things to do
than *play.* This is ridiculous! I've spent
the last forty-eight hours alone with you!"
I've made our idyll sound like an ordeal . . .

6

Like a middle-aged runner out of practice,
already apprehensive, short of wind
before she leaves the quarter-mark behind,
this aging writer cleaning up her act is
dubious she'll make the finish. Fact is
(though soaking in the sun she's disinclined
to pessimism) sparse in an untrained mind
which seethes on itself, unplanted, brackish
swamp-marsh. Still, there's enough clay mud
to mound with broken oyster-shells and sand
for a path between palm-swamp and marshland.
Sweaty and second-winded now, she jogs
over a creek bridged by uncertain logs.
Thud! leaving steady ooze-filled tread-marks, Thud!

"How come, here, you see so many black
people working in other people's houses?"
Does she notice, every other friend of ours is
ambiguous two generations back?
Like Bedouin for *sand,* or Eskimo
for *snow,* mixed races swell the lexicon,
peach-cream through copper to obsidian:
preta, negrinho, mulata, moreno.
Her café-au-lait father, olive mother
made her *rubia,* gold on lion-gold
like the naked sungilt three-year-old
who, crouched near a bloat sewer, ferreted
his hillside of the disinherited
looking enough like her to be her brother.

8
for Nélida Piñon

"How come," she says, "if you were what she is,
County Attorney, and someone did what
you thought they had a reason for, you've got
to say they're guilty? If you have the same ideas?
That boy—how could somebody say he is
going to learn anything in jail? He shot
the father 'cause he hurt his sister, not
to kill him!" Our polyglot host, child-free, is
charmed by such eloquence so late at night.
Iva waits, in Portuguese, to get
her lasagna. "It doesn't *taste* right."
The waiter brings a more familiar heap.
Stretching her four-foot-six on the banquette,
swiftly and righteously she falls asleep.

9
for Eleanor Bender

Out on the Dyckman Street platform because
there's no one else to fetch the magazine
mail from its distant post-box, something between
bag-lady, mountaineer, and Santa Claus,
I snort cold damp air, stamp to shift the weight
of twenty dozen women's manuscripts.
Twelve will, if merely literate, eclipse
the dismal two-hundred-and-twenty-eight
I'll read later—if the local arrives.
This is part of the world's work, I guess:
canceled subscriptions, invoices, housewives'
painstakingly misspelled longhand clichés.
(My cynicism is rebuked always.)
"Please send" (no stamps) "feedback to this address."

10

Now that she reads in bed till two A.M.
she does by dim pillow-lamps of hotel-
rooms in old towns whose names she cannot spell,
with walls around, churches centering them.
She won't go in museums, but will scale
any Romanesque or Gothic pile,
racing term-end outings of French school-
children sharing stretched possibles: a real
duke's birdcage dungeon straddling the south tower,
the sacristan's moquette beyond the bell
of vineyards, dollhouse fortress on a hill,
shadowed by pensive monsters who aspire
to the Lady's intercessive smile
as boats head slowly elsewhere up-canal.

She marched away, tagged "Unaccompanied Minor,"
and idiotically I felt like weeping,
although I didn't get any work done for
two weeks, except mornings when she was sleeping
late, her round brown face through dirty hair
clear as a Koré's, and for once not talking.
I tried to scribble at the town pool where
she swam, fair days or foul. Incessant walking
up steep hills to the back streets firmed up my
calves, lengthened my wind, and kept my blood-pressure
down. I needn't eat only where pizza
is served, or stockpile Limonade and Treets—a
small recompense. French kids on holiday
will hog the pool, and already I miss her.

12
for Nadja Tesich

Arching in heat, tabbies from the Mairie
wail contrapuntal to the Tramontane
on a high wall under a chestnut tree.
The named wind swept the twilight sky of rain-
clouds and scoured fog from the valley-bowl.
Above tiled roofs, schooled swallows bank and glide
on her apron-strings. Women inside
steep houses bar the shutters. On a knoll
knotty with sage and bramble, above vine-
rich fields, catching her breath, the seventy-
year-old hiker tears a garlicked roll,
re-caps her bottle and looks up the line
of hills as intimate as family
with whom she'll break more bread after nightfall.

13

The afternoon ahead of us seemed long.
I almost wished that it was dinnertime
(whenever I'm horny, I first think I'm
hungry) in prandial silence till, headstrong,
I'd interrupt the respirating wine
and, as I raised my glass, venture to raise
my eyes to her unsentimental gaze.
"—Let's see 'The Women Futurists'; that's fine."
A billboard in the Avenue de Maine
warned midnight as we wandered off the meal.
The night ahead of us was almost over
when, sweaty, she pulled me, sweaty, down to cover
her white-flagged brown chest on much-washed chenille.
She has a mother's coarsened breasts, like mine.

GRAFFITI FROM THE
GARE SAINT-MANQUÉ

GRAFFITI FROM THE
GARE SAINT-MANQUÉ

for Zed Bee

Outside the vineyard is a caravan
of Germans taking pictures in the rain.
The local cheese is Brillat-Savarin.
The best white wine is Savigny-les-Beaune.
We learn Burgundies while we have the chance
and lie down under cabbage-rose wallpaper.
It's too much wine and brandy, but I'll taper
off later. Who is watering my plants?
I may go home as wide as Gertrude Stein
—another Jewish Lesbian in France.

Around the sculptured Dukes of Burgundy,
androgynous monastics, faces cowled,
thrust bellies out in marble ecstasy
like child swimmers having their pigtails toweled.
Kids sang last night. A frieze of celebrants
circles the tomb, though students are in school,
while May rain drizzles on the beautiful
headlines confirming François Mitterand's
election. We have Reagan. Why not be
another Jewish Lesbian in France?
Aspiring Heads of State are literate
here, have favorite poets, can explain
the way structuralists obliterate
a text. They read at night. They're still all men.
Now poppy-studded meadows of Provence

blazon beyond our red sardine-can car.
We hope chairpersons never ask: why are
unblushing deviants abroad on grants?
My project budget listed: Entertain
another Jewish Lesbian in France.

I meant my pithy British village neighbor
who misses old days when sorority
members could always know each other: they wore
short-back-and-sides and a collar and tie.
She did, too. Slavic eyes, all romance
beneath an Eton crop with brilliantined
finger-waves, photographed at seventeen
in a dark blazer and a four-in-hand:
a glimpse of salad days that made the day for
another Jewish Lesbian in France.

Then we went on to peanuts and Campari,
she and her friend, my friend and I, and then
somehow it was nine-thirty and a hurry
to car and *carte* and a carafe of wine,
Lapin Sauté or Truite Meunière in Vence.
Convivial quartet of friends and lovers:
had anyone here dreaded any other's
tears, dawn recriminations and demands?
Emphatically not. That must have been
another Jewish Lesbian in France.

It's hard to be almost invisible.
You think you must be almost perfect too.
When your community's not sizeable,
it's often a community of two,
and a dissent between communicants
is a commuter pass to the abyss.
Authorities who claim you don't exist
would sometimes find you easy to convince.
(It helps if you can talk about it to
another Jewish Lesbian in France.)

A decorated she-Academician
opines we were thought up by horny males.
No woman of equivalent position
has yet taken the wind out of her sails.
(How would her "lifelong companion" have thanked her?)
Man loving Man's *her* subject, without mention
if what they do is due to her invention
—and if I'd been her mother, I'd have spanked her.
(Perhaps in a suppressed draft *Hadrian*'s
another Jewish Lesbian in France.)

Then the advocates of Feminitude
—with dashes as their only punctuation—
explain that Reason is to be eschewed:
In the Female Subconscious lies salvation.
Suspiciously like Girlish Ignorance,

it seems a rather watery solution.
If I can't dance, it's not my revolution.
If I can't think about it, I won't dance.
So let the ranks of *Psych et Po* include
another Jewish Lesbian in France.

I wish I had been packed off to the nuns
to learn good manners, Attic Greek, and Latin.
(No public Bronx Junior High School fit all that in.)
My angsts could have been casuistic ones.
It's not my feminist inheritance
to eat roots, drink leaf broth, live in a cave,
and not even know how to misbehave
with just one vowel and five consonants.
This patchwork autodidact Anglophone's
another Jewish Lesbian in France,

following Natalie Barney, Alice B.
Toklas, Djuna Barnes, generous Bryher,
Romaine Brooks, Sylvia Beach, H.D.,
Tamara de Lempicka, Janet Flanner.
They made the best use of the circumstance
that blood and stockings often both were bluish;
(they all were white, and only Alice Jewish)
wicked sept / oct / nonagenarians.
Would it have saved Simone Weil's life to be
another Jewish Lesbian in France?

It isn't sex I mean. Sex doesn't save
anyone, except, sometimes, from boredom
(and the underpaid under-class of whoredom
is often bored at work). I have a grave
suspicion ridicule of Continence
or Chastity is one way to disparage
a woman's choice of any job but marriage.
Most of us understand what we renounce.
(This was a lunchtime peptalk I once gave
another Jewish Lesbian in France

depressed by temporary solitude
but thinking coupled bliss was dubious.)
I mean: one way to love a body viewed
as soiled and soiling existential dross
is knowing through your own experience
a like body embodying a soul
to be admirable and loveable.
That is a source that merits nourishment.
Last night despair dressed as self-loathing wooed
another Jewish Lesbian in France.

The sheet was too soft. Unwashed for three weeks,
it smelled like both of us. The sin we are
beset by is despair. I rubbed my cheeks
against the cotton, thought, I wouldn't care
if it were just *my* funk. Despair expands

to fill . . . I willed my arm: extend; hand: stroke
that sullen shoulder. In the time it took
synapse to realize abstract commands,
the shoulder's owner fell asleep. Still there
another Jewish Lesbian in France

stared at the sickle moon above the skylight,
brooding, equally sullen, that alone
is better after all. As close as my right
foot, even my bed stops being my own.
Could I go downstairs quietly, make plans
for myself, not wake her? Who didn't undress,
slept on the couch bundled with loneliness
rather than brave that nuptial expanse
five weeks before. Another contradiction
another Jewish Lesbian in France

may reconcile more gracefully than I.
We're ill-equipped to be obliging wives.
The post office and travel agency
are significant others in our lives.
Last summer I left flowers at Saint Anne's
shrine. She had daughters. One who, legends tell,
adrift, woman-companioned, shored (is still
revered) in the Camargue, her holy band's
navigatrix, Mary, calming the sea
—another Jewish Lesbian in France?

It says they lived together forty years,
Mary and Mary and Sarah (who was black).
Unsaintly ordinary female queers,
we packed up and went separately back.
We'd shared the road with Gypsy sleeper vans
to join Sarah's procession to the shore.
Our own month-end anabasis was more
ambiguous. Among Americans
my polyglot persona disappears,
another Jewish Lesbian in France.

Coeur mis à nu in sunlight, khaki pants
I've rolled up in a beach towel so ants
and crickets from the leafage won't invade
their sweaty legs: in a loaned hermit-glade
pine-redolent of New Hampshire, not France,
I disentangle from the snares I laid.
Liver-lobed mushrooms thicken in the shade,
shrubs unwrap, pinelings thrust through mulch. Noon slants
across my book, my chest, its lemonade
rays sticky as a seven-year-old's hands.

THE SNOW QUEEN

THE WITCH'S GARDEN

*"For the old woman was a witch, but not a
wicked witch. She only used magic for her
own pleasure, and right now she very much
wanted Gerda to stay with her."*
H. C. Andersen: The Snow Queen

It is lucky for me she's
easy as a cat to please:
Have her morning cup in place.
Keep my hair out of my face.
Pick strawberries, save her some.
I can make myself at home.

If I do what she wants, and do it
lovingly, she'll love me. Who it
is I was or want or blunder
after she has dug in under
dung-ripe rows of mounded loam.
I can make myself at home.

It is heavy summer. I'm
cruel to remind her time
passes when she wants to stay

with me in the sun all day.
Berries swell, blooms droop, bees hum.
I can make myself at home.

If I cross her, she will cry.
She was lonelier than I
was, impatient while emphatic
April rain hammered the attic.
She is happy now I've come.
I can make myself at home.

Hugs and kisses, featherbed
blanket-stitched hard-candy red.
Nightlong windy leaves unravel
seams of roads I meant to travel.
Dressing table, mirror, comb:
I can make myself at home.

Some accretive secret grows
in the cave of what she knows,
like a rotting leaf-heap I
burn and scatter ash to scry
where to go when I have gone.
I can make myself at home.

WHAT THE TAME CROW SANG TO GERDA
for Judith de Karolyi

The Snow Queen had a daughter   la la   or two
She calls them and ignores them   but
They live in different countries   now
Her icy courtship drove them   out.

She names her selfish reasons   Reason.
Jeweled, she kept them dumb and hungry.   Good
Housekeepers, they can scry words scratched on   food.
In steamy bulwarks they survive her   season.

Old and spry, they both are almost   wise,
Ringed with hot stones, terrified of   waste.
Tears scalded her dream-ice from their   eyes.
Each smashed a glass, forgot a sister's   face.

They watch her frozen spires with yearning,   burn
With daughter-lust. Lost girl, you'll have your   turn.

GERDA IN THE EYRIE

*"Then the robber girl put her
arm round Gerda's neck and
slept. But Gerda was much too
afraid to close her eyes."*
H. C. Andersen: The Snow Queen

I almost love you. I've wanted to be you
all my life. You are asleep in the straw
with my story, your arm thrown across
my neck. Under your weight, I'm awake,
prickly-bladdered, listening to rooks
in the eaves. Your breath rasps,
fresher than the straw, across my face.
The texture of your skin is strange because
it's familiar. I felt vertigo,
nausea, when you touched my mouth with your
mouth, smelling of peat-smoke, then
vertigo took direction. I could have dived
into your dark.
              Do you have a story?
I imagine you always here, growing
with trees, testing your daily strength,
not exemplary, necessary. Corded
shoulders protect your brown new breasts
when you take off your stained embroidered shirt.
You wrapped yourself for sleep in the soft shawl
I had unknotted. Your breasts asked, like eyes.
A girl looks at another girl's breasts
covertly, thinking, we should be alike,

68

we are the same kind. But we are not.
Fear tethers me to the fire. I was raised afraid
of strange men, sudden noises, groups of men
in the square, isolate men on the road.
Alone in the woods, I never was alone
before. A drunk, a tinker, a bear
that meant a man, somebody's runaway
father or brother or son, would find me
expendable landscape. I'm following
a woman, now, alone. The trees
are simply trees and let me look at them.
What would a witch do to me, or a captious
princess? What a man does to a man;
nothing to make me cringe around the trees
again. The witch knew something I should know,
but I was in a hurry.
     Listen: worst
of all was, all along, I didn't mind.
I said I was the sinewy small girl
with tucked-up skirts, who was the general,
who made a boy eat dirt, who kept one doll
dressed as a pirate. Well, I had six
beribboned china ladies with real hair.
I asked for a new one each year. I pricked
flowers on cloth where someone else had drawn
them, with my back to the sun. I like
doing it, it made space in my mind
smooth as cream. I used diminutives,
collected miniatures. A tiny world

was what I played at, bottle-fed and tame.
You aren't listening. You're asleep
in your adventure, which I probably
won't know, maybe take part in. I won't know
what part. And this is in my head, where I
talk like a grown-up.
                    Grandma's little girl
talked like a grown-up: Wait and see; wait and see.
He was my twin self, my better brother.
That was my story, that I told myself
as puberty relentlessly divided
the tomboys from the boys. First we dress dolls,
then, confine cats, then, children
are handed over to caged children
who, every day, deck and affirm the cage.
When he laughed at me, I expected it.
When he dragged his sled to the boys' pond,
I watched, behind a tree. I could have asked
to go too. I was indulged. A girl
would be safe, playing with a band of boys,
from men. But I was happy where I was.
I listened to him whistling down the hill.
I thought about my hassock near the fire
to whose round seat my first embroidery,
maroon ground, daisies and a fleur-de-lys,
was tacked, sits still. I went in. I sat still.
So it was Kay the stranger lured away.
The woman stranger. If I find them, when I find her,
will she seize me like you did, with grubby

paws: "Nobody touch her, she's *mine!*"
A *girl* said that—you did—about a girl
—*me*. I guess you saved my life. Because
a girl said it, the danger couldn't be real.
That was what made me giggle. But it was.
I thought of something I heard from the witch.
You shut out images of what you fear:
your pupils pinhole; dilate when you're shown
what you desire. A picture of a gun
dilates men's eyes. Women's shrink. (From a niche
of crumbling mortar, you plucked your honed knife
and showed it to me shyly, like a jewel
saved for betrothal. Close to your curled hand
in warm straw, now it glistens as it sleeps.)
The image of a man—if women's eyes
contract; if they widen, shown a woman;
and men's do, too; would you have been surprised?
That means some of us fear what we desire,
and don't look at it with our entire
vision. I don't think I'm afraid of you,
though I should be, but I can't sleep, here.
I don't want to get up. What do you fear?
What do you want? Are they ever the same?
I want you to wake up and talk to me.
You're here, but you aren't really here.
Your elbow's getting heavy, like a stone
or a dead branch across my collarbone,
except it smells like you. The tiniest
shove, would you wake up? I know a game

we could play, or I could tell you a story.
You could tell one. If I turn on my side
with my back to you, your arm is around
me more lightly, a hug, and I can ride
to sleep on your lap, knees bent on your knees,
my arm over your arm under my breasts,
while your wild pets make early morning sounds.

THE ROBBER WOMAN

"Listen," said the Robber Girl
to Gerda, "you see that all the
robbers are gone. Only my
mother is left and she will
soon fall asleep. Then I shall
do something for you."
H. C. Andersen: The Snow Queen

I cuffed you into shape. I molded you
in my swelling matrix, pushed you out
into the world. I push you into the world
daily, and the labor is the same:
very like pain, unless I work at it.

As long as I sleep among thieves
you are safe in the upper air.

You kicked me from the inside long enough
when I bulged with you. I put my elbows
on what must have been your pointed butt
and watched your bony angles flying out.
I picked my load up when I'd caught my breath.

As long as I sleep among thieves
you are safe in the upper air.

I hug you and I slap you. I kiss you
and I curse you. I get your booted foot
on my scarred shins. I can still throw you down

and pick you up. Most of the time, it's play.
You knocked my knife-hand and my breath out today.

As long as I sleep among thieves
you are safe in the upper air.

You cheered when your head reached my belt-buckle.
Now I can't peer into your matted hair.
You lean against me. I can rest my chin
on your head, smelling unwashed child, while you
play-punch my breasts the way you always did.

As long as I sleep among thieves
you are safe in the upper air.

I always feel you in my hands, like clay.
You're oven-ready now. When you are baked
in the kiln of the world, my hands could break
what they made as accidentally
as easily as anybody's hands.

As long as I sleep among thieves
you are safe in the upper air.

You've started. I've scrubbed away your first blood.
My breasts are hard as when we nursed. I'm due.
You chose your friend; you took her for yourself

up into that cat-hideout where you sleep.
I hardly wonder what you talk about.

You are safe in the upper air
to believe what a child believes:
no blow that you receive
will ever leave a scar
but the impatient care-
less clout your mother gives;
certain that if you live
another hundred years
you never will forgive
a grain of malice there.
No harm ascends the stairs
unless your mother leaves
the bedroom door ajar.
The heavy step that weaves
its twist of fear in rev-
eries of empowered love
is—do you doubt it—hers.
The clean wind strips the eaves.
You stretch to what you will dare.
No one will know what you are
as long as I sleep among thieves.

THE LITTLE ROBBER GIRL
CONSIDERS THE WIDE WORLD

Far from the steamy parlors of the north,
aspiring rooftrees soar above the hearth.
Although they splay like courtiers' coolers, swards
of undergrowth clank in the wind like swords,

like that cloisonné fencing-master's skewer
mounted to proffer towels near the shower.
Whatever I can do, I'm going to do it,
with no one to forbid it or allow it.

I washed myself and washed myself. Blue tile
speculated on the ring I stole
while mispronouncing toasts with the entire
retinue of a People's Ambassador

who pinched my arm and reeled out such a line!
It's harder work than huddling in the cold.
I'm tired of eating all my meals alone,
glimpsing myself in silver like a child.

I can salvage without being foolish:
whatever tales her scraggly carrion birds
hear from my mother as she rocks and broods,
only my ankles and my wrists are girlish.

They said I'd bake to blazes, but they lied.
I think I never will be warm enough.
The noon sun satisfies my lizard blood.
I wish I hadn't given her my knife

because she didn't cry though I could bruise
her with my thumb. She doesn't know I loathe
her drool about an ice boy and a rose.
It was like stroking a blacksnake: too smooth.

She'd tell me better secrets if I pried.
Sooner or later, I'd get tired of bossing
her around. If I could tweak and prod
her to fight back, that would be appetizing—

except she went away early this morning,
saddle-strapped like a piglet on a spit.
(I can't ride horses well yet, but I'm learning.)
Beyond the egret's marsh, I found a spot . . .

Oh, I can't even make up a good story.
I stomp around the footpath, getting bitten
by gnats and kicking rocks and feeling rotten.
I'm bored, is all: it isn't so mysteri-

ous. It's hours and hours and hours till dinner.
I wish I had my knife. I bet she'll drop
it and lose it, or give it to that drip
and never use it for herself. Piss on her!

RUNE OF THE FINLAND WOMAN

for Sára Karig

*"You are so wise," the reindeer said, "you can
bind the winds of the world in a single strand."*
H. C. *Andersen:* The Snow Queen

She could bind the world's winds in a single strand.
She could find the world's words in a singing wind.
She could lend a weird will to a mottled hand.
She could wind a willed word from a muddled mind.

She could wend the wild woods on a saddled hind.
She could sound a well-spring with a rowan wand.
She could bind the wolf's wounds in a swaddling-band.
She could bind a banned book in a silken skin.

She could spend a world war on invaded land.
She could pound the dry roots to a kind of bread.
She could feed a road gang on invented food.
She could find the spare parts of the severed dead.

She could find the stone limbs in a waste of sand.
She could stand the pit cold with a withered lung.
She could handle bad puns in the slang she learned.
She could dandle foundlings in their mother tongue.

She could plait a child's hair with a fishbone comb.
She could tend a coal fire in the Arctic wind.

She could mend an engine with a sewing-pin.
She could warm the dark feet of a dying man.

She could drink the stone soup from a doubtful well.
She could breathe the green stink of a trench latrine.
She could drink a queen's share of important wine.
She could think a few things she would never tell.

She could learn the hand code of the deaf-and-blind.
She could earn the iron keys of the frozen queen.
She could wander uphill with a drunken friend.
She could bind the world's winds in a single strand.

THE LITTLE ROBBER GIRL
GETS ON IN THE WIDE WORLD
for Julie Fay

She's in a room full of letters, dressed in white
amidst proliferate papers, the exploded lace of sheets.
Her hair froths white, her pale eyes chill, as when I first
saw her. Under white trouser-legs, her long feet

are bare on the stone floor, swollen with heat.
Summer follows summer since the first time
I stood in her crepuscular bedroom
awaiting acknowledgement. The dim chime

of a blue glass clock caught her attention. "I'm
exhausted. Come at six tomorrow. Knock
downstairs. I'll hear you. The heat makes me sick.
Debarrass me of that ridiculous clock."

I put it in my pocket. I left the lock
unlatched. Who knows what I thought I'd do?
I watched from a huge-boled olive tree, her window
a tall candle, while dusk deepened, blue

as my road clothes, and a blade of new
moon sharpened above the limestone bluffs.
"I knew where you were last night. I heard you laugh."
Her sight is dim, but her ears are sharp enough.

I thought, "Let her be captious, she's a tough
old bird, and, say what you like, she deserves

a bit of courtesy. While I'm here, I won't starve.
You're not a slave when you contract to serve."

I don't know when it was I lost my nerve.
I was delighted when she seemed to trust
me. I brought the right coins back, her birdscratch list
transformed to fill the larder. Late in the August

heat, shadowed by shutters, we discussed
my future and her past. Sometimes they blended
to one chivalric tale. I understand it
a little better now. She would make splendid

generous gestures in which I pretended
to believe. If it were hers to give,
she'd give it to me—what? her land, her glove
to carry, the bracelet under her sleeve?

Pretended? why? She didn't want me to leave;
she told me so in several languages,
while I continued to sleep under her trees,
presenting myself mornings, neatly dressed

as I could manage. Each day was a new test.
She sent me out and always I came back
with packages, messages. "You bring me good luck."
I had good luck, I thought. I had a knack

for pleasing. The blue glass clock lived in my rucksack.
Afternoons, I wrote letters, a diligent steward,
weeded the moribund garden while it parched,
stood barefoot on cool tiles while she descended

the tortuous stairway, her gnarled hand extended
toward me. Did I say, she was beautiful,
that youth, in her scintillant pallor, paled
to decorative nursery pastel?

I felt large, rude and bland, all the more grateful,
though my food and outdoor shelter were all my wages.
Blackberry clumps weighted the brambly hedges.
Sometimes I thought of winter hills' blank pages

scrawled with one bird-track. I forgot my real age—is
that strange? and that once I was almost always cold.
Brown rabbits and grey water-rats ran wild
in the hedges. No animal should be killed

on her land, she said. My nights outdoors were filled
with rustlings, scrabblings. I thought about rats
and rolled down, shivering, into my blankets.
"Womanish," she mocked, when I told her that.

I plunged my face into a fresh-washed sheet
as I lifted it to hang. The odor
of wet linen enveloped unthought-of tears.
I never had done woman's work before

but now I did it daily, over and over.
Sometimes I was insulted, as no servant
who'd take her pay and leave would be. I didn't.
Sometimes I was her twilight confidante,

gallant, or granddaughter, or sycophant.
She liked me best when I was brusque and lewd.
If I was timid, she would call me stupid,
but she'd laugh and correct a misconstrued

sentence I almost halfway understood.
The sun set earlier, but we sat late. Around her
shoulders, I wrapped her black-barred cloak. She was fonder
of talk than fire. Meanwhile the magpies, sometimes the thunder,

meanwhile the footpath wound serpentine under
the bushes, tucked in around limestone boulders
above the river-sectioned slopes where wilder
things wandered in the night as I got older,

and she, chameleon, stayed the same, I told her.
Meanwhile the trail debouched on a small road
that led—although I didn't know where it led—
somewhere. From our hill, it was hidden by woods.

After a storm, mist marked the bluffs: it showed.
Meanwhile I scrabbled weeds where no one reaped.
Harvest was windfall. Greengages the wasps
ate splattered tree-roots, or heaped

in their forks, a rats' feast while we slept.
Smashed yellow pears fermented in the grass
the afternoon I thought I'd cut my losses.
With a soiled shirt-sleeve, I rubbed the milk-glass

clock till my face glimmered back from its facets.
I wrapped my four garments around it, rolled
them in my blanket. I stripped her down-drowned bed
of its champagne-silk crewelwork. I sold

that to a market-woman. Well, I thought of it, told
myself I ought, might, was entitled to,
as I tied up the rucksack. *Do you know,
that's probably what she expects of you?*

So I turn, part hedges, shield my eyes. I go
up to my haunches in persistent brambles.
Nobody promised me it would be simple.
Nobody's future passes out free samples.

Sunbeams stroked me at a farewell angle
while the watchlight in my mind's eye sought her
shadow smiting rock with an olive mitre:
"You are a thief, and a thief's daughter!"

THE LITTLE ROBBER GIRL
CONSIDERS SOME OPTIONS

Who wouldn't love the bad old ladies? I'd rather not go gaga in a
nursing home, or be preserved in plastic slipcovers with a sullen home
attendant paid by a despicable son-in-law. If I can't grow sinewy on a
hillside with my twenty years' mostly companion, selling books, pots
or rocks in a shop and sitting to three healthy courses on the precise
stroke of nine, then I could be captious in a crooked castle, more courted
a ruin than ever I was a *rouée*, avid for gossip and close with my favor.
The third choice, only granted as a reward, is to pack the gold hero's
medal and the ornamental sword in a battered briefcase with one drip-
dry shirt, and set out, on the very eve of your triumphal fireworks, to
char in the ice dame's half-dismantled mansion, to bind the enemy's
atlas with your last silk ball-gown, to tell bedtime stories to the torturer
who brings you cream teas, and to the orphans for whom you butchered
a horse with the ceremonial epée. Then your digestion will rival your
memory, your breasts will grow back while you learn Catalan, and
your daughters slog across the icecap to get drunk with you.

BALLAD OF LADIES
LOST AND FOUND

BALLAD OF LADIES
LOST AND FOUND
for Julia Alvarez

Where are the women who, *entre deux guerres,*
came out on college-graduation trips,
came to New York on football scholarships,
came to town meeting in a decorous pair?
Where are the expatriate *salonnières,*
the gym teacher, the math-department head?
Do nieces follow where their odd aunts led?
The elephants die off in Cagnes-sur-Mer.
H.D., whose "nature was bisexual,"
and plain old Margaret Fuller died as well.

Where are the single-combat champions:
the Chevalier d'Eon with curled peruke,
Big Sweet who ran with Zora in the jook,
open-handed Winifred Ellerman,
Colette, who hedged her bets and always won?
Sojourner's sojourned where she need not pack
decades of whitegirl conscience on her back.
The spirit gave up Zora; she lay down
under a weed-field miles from Eatonville,
and plain old Margaret Fuller died as well.

Where's Stevie, with her pleated schoolgirl dresses,
and Rosa, with her permit to wear pants?
Who snuffed Clara's *mestiza* flamboyance

and bled Frida onto her canvases?
Where are the Niggerati hostesses,
the kohl-eyed ivory poets with severe
chignons, the rebels who grew out their hair,
the bulldaggers with marcelled processes?
Conglomerates co-opted Sugar Hill,
and plain old Margaret Fuller died as well.

Anne Hutchinson, called witch, termagant, whore,
fell to the long knives, having tricked the noose.
Carolina María de Jesús'
tale from the slagheaps of the landless poor
ended on a straw mat on a dirt floor.
In action thirteen years after fifteen
in prison, Eleanor of Aquitaine
accomplished half of Europe and fourscore
anniversaries for good or ill,
and plain old Margaret Fuller died as well.

Has Ida B. persuaded Susan B.
to pool resources for a joint campaign?
(Two Harriets act a pageant by Lorraine,
cheered by the butch drunk on the IRT
who used to watch me watch her watching me;
We've notes by Angelina Grimké Weld
for choral settings drawn from the *Compiled
Poems* of Angelina Weld Grimké.)
There's no such tense as Past Conditional,
and plain old Margaret Fuller died as well.

Who was Sappho's protégée, and when did
we lose Hrotsvitha, dramaturge and nun?
What did bibulous Suzanne Valadon
think about Artemisia, who tended
to make a life-size murderess look splendid?
Where's Aphra, fond of dalliance and the pun?
Where's Jane, who didn't indulge in either one?
Whoever knows how Ende, Pintrix, ended
is not teaching Art History at Yale,
and plain old Margaret Fuller died as well.

Is Beruliah upstairs behind the curtain
debating Juana Inés de la Cruz?
Where's *savante* Anabella, Augusta-Goose,
Fanny, Maude, Lidian, Freda and Caitlin,
"without whom this could never have been written"?
Louisa who wrote, scrimped, saved, sewed, and nursed,
Malinche, who's, like all translators, cursed,
Bessie, whose voice was hemp and steel and satin,
outside a segregated hospital,
and plain old Margaret Fuller died as well.

Where's Amy, who kept Ada in cigars
and love, requited, both country and courtly,
although quinquagenarian and portly?
Where's Emily? It's very still upstairs.
Where's Billie, whose strange fruit ripened in bars?
Where's the street-scavenging Little Sparrow?
Too poor, too mean, too weird, too wide, too narrow:

Marie Curie, examining her scars,
was not particularly beautiful;
and plain old Margaret Fuller died as well.

Who was the grandmother of Frankenstein?
The Vindicatrix of the Rights of Woman.
Madame de Sévigné said prayers to summon
the postman just as eloquent as mine,
though my Madame de Grignan's only nine.
But Mary Wollstonecraft had never known
that daughter, nor did Paula Modersohn.
The three-day infants blinked in the sunshine.
The mothers turned their faces to the wall;
and plain old Margaret Fuller died as well.

Tomorrow night the harvest moon will wane
that's floodlighting the silhouetted wood.
Make your own footnotes; it will do you good.
Emeritae have nothing to explain.
She wasn't very old, or really plain—
my age exactly, volumes incomplete.
"The life, the life, will it never be sweet?"
She wrote it once; I quote it once again
midlife at midnight when the moon is full
and I can almost hear the warning bell
offshore, sounding through starlight like a stain
on waves that heaved over what she began
and truncated a woman's chronicle,
and plain old Margaret Fuller died as well.

A NOTE ON THE AUTHOR

Marilyn Hacker was born in the Bronx on Thanksgiving
Day, 1942. Her first book, *Presentation Piece*, received the
National Book Award in 1975, and was a Lamont Poetry
Selection of the Academy of American Poets. She is also the
author of *Separations* (1976), and *Taking Notice* (1980),
whose title sequence was also published as a chapbook by Out
& Out Books. She was awarded a Guggenheim Fellowship
in 1980–81, and an Ingram-Merrill Foundation Fellowship
for 1984–85.

    She lives in Manhattan with her daughter, Iva, and is the
editor of the feminist literary magazine *13th Moon*.

A NOTE ON THE TYPE

The text of this book was set on the Linotype in a type face
known as Garamond. The design is based on letter forms
originally created by Claude Garamond (c.1480–1561).
Garamond was a pupil of Geoffroy Tory and may have pat-
terned his letter forms on Venetian models. To this day, the
type face that bears his name is one of the most attractive used
in book composition, and the intervening years have caused
it to lose little of its freshness or beauty.

Composed by Heritage Printers, Inc., Charlotte, North Carolina.
Printed and bound by Halliday Lithographers, Hanover,
Massachusetts.

Designed by Amy Berniker.